Praise for
Awaken Your Purpose

"Reading Jeanne Marie's book is like sitting with a trusted friend and having a meaningful conversation about how we choose to live our lives. From tapping into your creativity to realizing your limitless potential, this book will make you feel better about yourself, your purpose, and your life. It is both challenging and comforting and is a delight to read. Highly recommend!"

— **Joe Calloway**
Author of *Becoming a Category of One*

"It's rare to find a coach and mentor who helps you have a break-through in every single coaching interaction. I'm so impressed that Jeanne-Marie provides exactly that! She has been my coach and mentor for the past several years. As someone who has hired coaches for over two decades, I will say she is hands-down the most knowledgeable and impactful coach I've ever had."

— **Liz Sears**
Broker and CEO of Utah's Elite | REALTORS®at REAL Broker, LLC

"Jeanne-Marie's book has a wonderful way of keeping the reader engaged. She provides exercises and stories throughout, to keep you 'in the game' and thinking about what's most important to you."

— **Todd A. Finkle, Ph.D.**
Author of *Warren Buffett: Investor and Entrepreneur*

"Jeanne-Marie's contribution played a significant role in the grand success of our Mastermind Conference. Her astute observations of the audience enabled her to tailor her techniques to the needs of each individual. We were pleasantly surprised by the results, and highly recommend her services."

— Kristopher Ontiveros
CEO of Build a Better Phoenix

"Jeanne Marie is dynamic in her coaching. Her nonintimidating approach creates the opportunity for you to grow; folks were jumping out of their seats to participate and share!"

— William W. Predebon, Jr.
CEO of Creative Solutions Investments, LLC

"Working with Jeanne-Marie, I discovered innovative processes for handling problems. I learned to shift my focus from problem to solution. She brings all of herself to every situation, from coaching calls to business meetings. Jeanne-Marie will bring about the change you want in your world."

— Amy Sullivan Ryan
Owner and CFO of Arrowhead Auto Sales;
Co-host of *Everything and JACK Podcast*

"You can absolutely take your purpose to the next level, and Jeanne-Marie can help. She intuitively guides the conversation that needs to happen, so that you can see in your heart what's most important to you."

— Russ and Teri Flory
Top-Producing Real Estate Agents and Investors

"Como empresaria con múltiples compañías a nivel mundial, he experimentado el profundo impacto de trabajar con la 'High Performance Coach' Jeanne Marie durante más de 5 años. Cada conversación con ella genera una clara intención y propósito en mi vida, implementando herramientas vitales que han transformado mi mentalidad, influenciando positivamente mi palabra y compromiso en mi entorno y comunidades. Participar en el programa *The Ten Conversations™*, que lidera en nuestras empresas ha sido revelador, observando cómo influye en nuestros líderes y en quienes participan en otros programas, generando responsabilidad y toma de decisiones que impactan tanto en lo personal como en lo profesional, marcando una diferencia significativa en áreas como el producto final, la economía, las finanzas y los resultados como líderes."

— Sumary Oehlman Centeno
Founder and Human Development Director of Learn and Grow Rich

"She has given me hidden gems of knowledge. Imagine living in a world where you are guided by your commitments, regardless of your circumstances. That is a glimpse of what it's been like having Jeanne-Marie as my coach."

— **Umaer Haq**
CEO of Hands On Real Estate; Family Man; Business Coach

"It has been great participating in the international *Ten Conversations*™ series. My coach Jeanne-Marie has been a blessing and an encouragement to my life. I am forever impacted by her first statement to me: 'If you succeed, we all succeed; and if you fail, we all fail.'"

— **Captain Joseph Lemayan**
Evangelist in the Anglican Church of Kenya;
Teacher in the Maasai community

"Coaching with Jeanne-Marie is a guaranteed breakthrough every time! I have never had such a consistent and committed coach. She's not concerned with how you feel about her; she is concerned with how you feel about your *life*. And she's willing to push you and challenge a belief to get you to the other side."

— **Shannon Olsen**
CEO of My Utah Agents, My Idaho Agents, My Utah Stagers;
Keynote Speaker; Podcast host

"Jeanne Marie is an excellent high-performance coach who encourages transformation in every conversation. By working with her, I have had amazing success personally and with my team. This book is transformational and points you in the right direction."

— Angi Bair
Founder and CEO of Investing in Life, LLC;
Real Estate Broker; Real Estate Investor; Coach

"Jeanne-Marie's unique ability to interrupt limiting conversations has allowed me to break free from my self-imposed barriers and unlock my unlimited capacity in life and business. Through her guidance, I've gained profound clarity in my goals, and I've identified and overcome obstacles I didn't realize were holding me back.

Her coaching program *The Ten Conversations™*, as well as her role as a performance coach for my newly formed initiative, Lady Boss Alliance, have provided invaluable insights and strategies that have reshaped my approach to effectively executing our goals. She has a remarkable talent for making everyone feel seen and heard, and her commitment to helping others discover their authentic self-expression is evident.

In conclusion, Jeanne-Marie Eayrs is much more than a high-performance coach. She is a catalyst for change, and an advocate for personal growth. My journey with her has been transformative, and I am deeply grateful for her positive impact on my life."

— Caroline Skrdla, Ph.D.
Founder and CEO of Lady Boss Alliance;
Author; Speaker; Teacher; Podcaster

Awaken Your Purpose

Awaken Your Purpose

Beyond the Transaction

Jeanne-Marie Eayrs

EXPERT AUTHORITY EFFECT™ PUBLISHING

Detroit

AWAKEN YOUR PURPOSE

Beyond the Transaction

© 2024 Jeanne-Marie Eayrs

Published by Expert Authority Effect™ Publishing, an imprint of IWDNow Marketing L.L.C.

For information about permission to reproduce sections from this book, email: AwakenYourPurpose24@gmail.com

eBook ISBN: 978-1-957699-14-1
Paperback ISBN: 978-1-957699-15-8
Hardcover ISBN: 978-1-957699-16-5
Audiobook ISBN: 978-1-957699-17-2

10 9 8 7 6 5 4 3 2 1
1st Edition, March 2024

Printed in the United States of America

This book is dedicated to

Raeanna Marie Jane Pittman

&

Meghan Kali McNeil

DOWNLOAD THE AUDIOBOOK!

I wanted to make this the best book possible,
so I professionally recorded the accompanying audiobook.

TO DOWNLOAD GO TO:

www.JeanneMarieEayrs.com/AYPAudioBonus

Acknowledgments

I would like to acknowledge my incredibly supportive husband, Tim Ludlow, without whom I'd still be staring at the skinny branches.

Without my coach, Bill Allen, I'd still be complaining ... about nothing.

A shout out to Maura Gallucci and Ken Wertz, who patiently listened to me for hours on the phone and helped me move my book from thoughts to paper, line by line.

Then there are those wonderful friends and mentors who have gently pushed me to the finish line. You know who you are.

Thanks to my daughter, Raeanna Pittman, and my stepsons, Marko and Ivan Ludlow, who have been an encouragement from the beginning.

Also, much gratitude to my clients who have given me a purpose bigger than myself: For you to thrive and live amazing lives.

Thanks to Mario Fachini, of Expert Authority Effect™ Publishing, who calmly and patiently kept me on the path, when all I wanted to do was quit.

Thank you all for the loving support in writing my first book.

Contents

Foreword

If you are reading this, I want to personally congratulate you on taking a step forward in your life.

As someone who has been coached by Jeanne-Marie weekly for over five years, I have some simple words of advice: Strap in, hold on, and get ready for the time of your life. I say this because I have personally accomplished my 5-year goals in less than six months after starting to work with her. I have accomplished my 10-year goals in less than two years.

When I was eighteen years old, I had three things that were important to me:

1. Traveling the world
2. Helping people
3. Making a lot of money

I am personally writing this from an amazing resort in Bali, Indonesia, and have spent the last three years traveling full time to twenty-three countries with my amazing wife. We have epic adventures, helping countless people every day, and are making more money than we have ever made before.

Through coaching with Jeanne-Marie, I have discovered something money can't buy: peace of mind, and the ability to live in the present moment. I have also learned that I am enough and it will all work out. I believe this is important to know and understand because in my profession as a business owner and entrepreneur, I am going into the "unknown" daily. I need to have the confidence and conviction that I have what it takes to get through it, no matter what. This confidence and conviction has also transcended throughout my team. Now they also have even more confidence in me, and the vision that we are creating.

Over the years of working with Jeanne-Marie, I have built a team of over forty-five people in over twelve countries that run all of my businesses while I am traveling the world. It all started with Jeanne-Marie asking me one simple question: Why can't you have it all?

- Why can't you travel and grow your businesses?

- Why can't you have motorcycle rides and work?

- Why can't you do it all?

I knew anything I responded with would be coming from a space of fear and not being enough. That is what Jeanne-Marie is a master at — getting you to see you have everything you need right now to accomplish what you want. She doesn't tolerate the small thinking we all are used to. She challenges you in all aspects of your life, but she does it for you because that is what her coaching is about — making sure you are living an amazing life in all aspects of your life.

Not only is she a coach, but she embodies what it means to be a coach. She is constantly taking on her life to make sure she is living an exciting and empowered life, and she personally has a coach that she works with to make sure of it. She is the tip of the spear when it comes to showing people what is possible and showing them that if you want something, you can have it. Anything else is an excuse because that is how she lives her life. Jeanne-Marie works personally with my wife and me to make sure we stay empowered around our businesses and our marriage.

Jeanne-Marie is always a phone call away when we feel stuck and want to quit. She always knows what to say to get us back on track. It might be something inspirational, a personal story of how she had to overcome something similar, something loving, a high five, or a slap in the face (metaphorically speaking) to wake us up to who we really are and what we are committed to.

We brought Jeanne-Marie in to coach our entire team, and have been using *The Ten Conversations™* program, facilitated by Jeanne-Marie, for several years. We incorporated this because my wife and I are growing and evolving so quickly that we need those around us to keep growing with us. We need to make sure our team is also accomplishing their goals and living an empowered life. I only know one person who is up for the task of empowering forty-five-plus people in twelve countries, and that is Jeanne-Marie Eayrs.

Starting as my coach, she has grown into a trusted advisor, friend, and world travel partner. She, along with her husband Tim, are examples of what it means to constantly be pursuing the next thing and living life to the fullest. Jeanne-Marie believes life is lived on the court, and that is the only place she coaches you on. So, if you want to play life full-out and accomplish everything you want ...

Strap in, hold on, and get ready for the time of your life.

— Zach Oehlman

Founder and CEO, Learn and Grow Rich
LearnandGrowRich.net

Prologue

This book is arranged into *Five Foundational Frameworks™*. These frameworks, together with the accompanying exercises, will yield the best results for you. Here's a preview of the *Five Foundational Frameworks.*

Origin

In this chapter, we explore the nature of *transactions* and *purpose* in our lives.

Community

In this chapter, we look at the roles you play in your communities.

Business of Real Estate

In this chapter, you discover that you have more support than you know.

Money

In this chapter, we put money in its place.

Legacy

In this chapter, you get to design a legacy that reflects what's important to you.

It is so easy to get lost in the offers, the emails, the details in the contracts. These *Five Foundational Frameworks* provide guidance as you awaken your purpose.

Origin

Chapter 1

The First Foundational Framework

"We're in the middle of the greatest feat ever attempted. This is science's chance to be daring. What are you doing? Standing around, bitchin'."

From the movie *The Dish*

Wake Up! Welcome to awakening your purpose.

This is not a book of tips and tricks. Instead, it's an opportunity for you to enjoy the journey, from uncertainty to fully owning your purpose. It may feel daunting; but give yourself full permission to be in the unknown.

Think back to a time when you started something new. Do you remember all the excitement you felt at the beginning? But then, all too often, you hit the "resistance" phase. You probably recognize the telltale signs of resistance. Instead of working on the task at hand, you find all kinds of "important" things to do: go shopping; look at the leftovers in the fridge; binge-watch the latest Netflix series; have another cocktail, take a nap, start an argument; and one of my all-time favorites, rearrange the living room furniture.

Resistance isn't bad. You just want to observe yourself when resistance comes up. Believe me, I spent a lot of time swimming in resistance when I decided to write this book — *just ask my publisher!*

In this book, I intend to support you in breaking through some of your resistance. First, why do you want to awaken your purpose? What are you committed to in your life? When is the last time you asked yourself what you want in your life? When is the last time you talked with someone else about what you want in your life? We will explore these questions throughout this book. But for now, **STOP**.

Make a list of five things that you are committed to right now. This could include commitments such as family, health, career, spirituality, or whatever immediately comes to mind.

1 ____

2 ____

3 ____

4 ____

5 ____

Keep this list. This is to remind you what is important to you. We will be working throughout the next several chapters to find out what you really want and what you are here for. You may even want to consider what's next for you in your career, your marriage, and your life. Now, before we go any further, I do think it is important to remind you: While you are reading this book, you might find yourself occasionally feeling confronted, or sad. You might start complaining or feeling rebellious. Again, it is perfectly fine to experience resistance.

The Sun's Purpose

When I first moved to Arizona, I was struck by the extraordinary beauty of the sunrise. I've visited many countries around the world, so I've seen the sunrise from many latitudes and longitudes. But I do find something unique, something awe-inspiring, about the Arizona sunrise. If you want a glimpse of what I'm talking about, just look at the front cover of this book. It's a photograph I took from my balcony, and I love how it captures the radiance of the morning sun.

But if we look beyond the aesthetics, what can we say about the sun's purpose? The sun's purpose is to sustain us, by providing us with heat and light. It is essential for all living things, from the lowly worm to the mighty oak. As we here on Earth revolve around the sun, we rely on that glorious star, each day, to fulfill its purpose. Imagine your purpose being that powerful, beautiful, and inspiring.

Purpose of Language

In my twenties, I was in therapy, talking about my childhood and confronting my future. I was depressed, and I was seriously questioning what I was going to do for the rest of my life. On the one hand, I had already developed several talents: dancing, singing, playing piano, and painting; I was even dabbling with learning the alto saxophone. But, on the other hand, I had no idea how to use those talents. My therapist, who had an uncanny resemblance to Sigmund Freud, listened intently as I discussed my career pursuits. "You know," he said, holding his pen as if he was about to take a puff out of a pipe, "It's like you know how to speak many languages ... but you have nothing to say."

As you read this book, you might be at a crossroads in your career, or you might have found that the role you've been playing has run its course. At times like this, you might feel like you don't know how to put your purpose into words. Nonetheless, you have many talents and skills. Use this book to connect to those best parts of you. Without a deep appreciation of who you are in the world, you have nothing to say.

I recently stayed in the small Italian town of Casale Monferrato, which is situated between Turin and Milan. I felt lost because I did not speak Italian. I was not even able to describe the kind of shoes I needed at the local store. I so wanted to be connected to the local community. But without language, I had no connection.

Language comes in many forms. For example, numbers have an immense power to communicate, and even to affect your emotions. What is the emotion you have when you look at your credit score? Or how do you feel when you step on the scale, and look at that number between your feet? Have you ever had an intense reaction when you get the bill from your contractor? Notice how often you allow numbers to dictate your life.

When walking through the Royal Botanical Gardens during one of my trips to Melbourne, Australia, I noticed a large green sign that read *"WOMINJEKA".* It was a sign that translated to *"Welcome"* in the language of Australia's aboriginal Wurundjeri people.

WOMINJEKA

WOMIN — *to come from somewhere*

DJI — *I'm instructing you to come*

KA — *purpose*

This led me to a wonderful conversation with my dear friend, Stephen Morey, an Associate Professor in the Department of Languages and Cultures at La Trobe University in Melbourne. I asked Stephen whether the word *purpose* exists in all languages.

"The issue you raise is complex and I can think quickly of several things to say. One question is whether the function of *purpose* is encoded in a language; is there a word, a case ending for it? All languages will have a way of expressing *purpose* but not necessarily encoded. Thus, English has the word *for* — but *for* can also be a *beneficiary* (e.g. I baked a cake for my Mum). And the word *to* can be used for *purpose*. Then we need to ask if purpose is an underlying, necessary category in language."

The first steps of our journey together will include looking more closely at what purpose is, and what purpose is not. However, keep in mind that you are not actually *looking* for your purpose, but rather you are *rediscovering* your purpose.

Intention

While in Melbourne sitting outside a café, I started watching a small group of people chatting to each other. This was a perfect opportunity for people-watching, a perfect low-energy activity for a tourist. Slowly I became aware of the resignation and the general malaise of some of the people around me.

Nearby, there was a dog sitting by the side of an older gentleman. The dog was attentive and in quiet obedience. This little fella was waiting for his owner's direction. The dog was observing his surroundings and ready for the next command.

At a moment's notice, your dog will lovingly give you the attention you desperately need. Its purpose, being your best friend and companion for life, is non-negotiable. Witnessing these scenes sparked thoughts of purpose and intentions. Let's introduce you to your intentions.

If you don't have an *intention*, there is no way to measure your results. An intention is a moment-by-moment phenomenon. It is created from moment to moment.

Intention expresses a commitment to achieving specific outcomes. It reflects a conscious desire to bring about particular results. Intention requires ongoing self-observation.

Examples of intentions could include:

- My intention is to increase my level of performance.
- My intention is to have others be heard.
- My intention is to create a community.
- My intention is to feel accomplished.
- My intention is to have an intention.

So you are now looking for and focused solely on your intention. Once you have created an intention, you can then engage in purposeful actions.

Follow Instructions

Let's imagine you are in front of a building with three sets of double doors. You can walk through any door you choose. But you see everyone else walking through the double doors to the right. So you follow too. There you were with three possibilities available to you. But you "fell asleep" and had no intention but to follow everyone else.

You can observe this kind of behavior all around you. Have you noticed: When people are following instructions, they don't really have an intention other than following the instructions. Go to the exit, follow the leader, sign your name here, or sit down. It's a kind of sleepwalking. Here's a way to keep yourself awake: While following the instructions, ask yourself, "What is my intention right now?"

Transactions

This book is not about telling you what is good and bad, or right and wrong. It's about looking for the possibility of something beyond the transaction. It's about confronting the reality that you are living a transactional life. With that said, let's identify transactions.

Examples of transactions:

- Purchasing this book
- Filling your car with fuel
- Waving *"hello"* to a neighbor

- Ordering food at a restaurant
- Going through security at the airport
- Purchasing travel tickets online

Now, here's an opportunity for you to get present to the mass of transactions in your daily life.

Begin to speculate about the transactions you've been engaged with this week, and write them in the space below.

____

____

____

____

You might notice from this exercise how much you are driven by transactions. They are automatic. But that does not mean that there's anything wrong with transactions; we just need to recognize them for what they are.

The problem is not the transaction itself; the problem is thinking that the transaction is your purpose.

The Path to Purpose

When creating your purpose, you will be going beyond the transaction and accessing a pathway to something greater than yourself. However, we do want to address certain "imposters" along the way. These imposters are common tasks and activities that people often mistake for their purpose.

Let's take a brief look at some of these tasks and activities:

- A mission
- A vision
- A task
- A goal
- A transaction
- A project

For example, think about cleaning out your garage. Is that a purpose? No, that is considered a task. It might be a task that you've worked on for ten years. It might even feel like it's becoming a mission. Nonetheless, it is a task.

What about raising funds for the homeless? If this calls to you, certainly keep doing what you're doing. But don't mistake this great project for a purpose.

How about traveling to Indonesia? Nope, that is a goal.

There is nothing wrong with any of these. They are all great ideas. However, they are not your purpose.

Are You Ready?

I designed a coaching program called *The Ten Conversations™*, which I deliver to groups of people via video call. Typically, at the beginning of the first session, I ask the attendees, "Are you ready?" This simple question reveals a lot about the people who are attending the program.

One person shouts out, "Ready for what?" Another apologizes for being late. One annoyed person calls out from behind a blank screen "I need to get my notebook."

I allow this to play out for a bit. Then I ask again, "Are you ready?" By this time, a few (but not all) of the attendees raise their hands to signal Yes. And then someone asks, "When are we starting?"

My answer is always the same: "For those of you wondering when we are starting, we already started."

As you progress through this book, remember that you already started. You started the moment you were born.

The Power of Context

I remember coaching one of my clients, a real estate agent named Paul. He complained about how he had to go door-to-door prospecting for new clients. "I knocked on sixty doors today; what a waste of my time," he said. Although any single one of those sixty doors might have resulted in a six-figure payday, Paul could not see a positive way to look at the situation. It just seemed like hard work to him.

However, as I listened to his complaint, my intention was to empower him to love his job. "Well," I began, "Is there another way of going door to door?" He looked a little perplexed, "I don't know, it's just something I have to do." I decided to dig in, and I asked if he had any kids. "Yes," he replied. "Ok, so how do your kids go door to door on Halloween?" I asked. He thought about it for a second, and said, "They spend several weeks thinking about what they are going to wear. Then on Halloween, they go from door to door filling up their pillowcases with candy."

Paul saw that he could shift his context from "hard work" to a child's perspective of capturing as much candy as possible. That sounds like a lot more fun!

What would happen if you applied the same enthusiasm to your business?

Declaration

"We choose to go to the moon in this decade and do the other things, not because they are easy, but because they are hard."
John. F. Kennedy

The moment I declared, "I am writing a book", I stopped waiting. I took action.

In much the same way, after President Kennedy delivered his address at Rice University in 1962, declaring the goal of putting man on the moon, the United States stopped waiting. Over 400,000 NASA personnel took action.

Where does your purpose come from? For many, their purpose springs from calamities, catastrophes, or tragedies. However, you don't have to wait for the sea to part or the skies to open. You can declare your purpose at any time, any place, for any reason. Your purpose is already within you. Now, are you ready to declare it?

What Comes Naturally

When I was ten years old, my best friend, Alison Waren, and I were inseparable. Alison was clever, funny, and talented; best of all, everyone liked her. I am not sure whether Alison was in a marching band, but she sure knew how to twirl a baton. In school, we talked incessantly and giggled a lot. We practiced cartwheels, handstands, and leapfrog during recess.

Each day after school, we would walk each other home. First, I walked Alison to her house. But we found that we hadn't quite finished talking about all the things that matter to 10-year-old girls. So Alison walked me back to my house. And as we walked back and forth from my house to hers, we eventually, reluctantly parted ways, knowing we would do it all again tomorrow.

Today, as a coach, I find myself metaphorically walking people home.

My cowboy friend, Chris Rich, went on his first camping trip with his dad at four years old. His father introduced him to fishing at Christopher's Creek in Arizona. He would watch the fish swimming and wait hours and hours for a fish to bite at the end of his rod. Eventually, one of those fish bit, and in that moment, WHAM, Chris said, his life changed forever. "I got one! I got one! I got one!" he yelled as he ran through the campground. Nothing else mattered more than catching a fish to that four-year-old boy.

I spoke to Chris recently about his passion for fishing. I asked him whether fishing was one of those natural expressions for him. Chris's response surprised me, "It's not the fish I'm after; it is the connection to my friends, family, my dad, the great outdoors, and traveling all over the world while I am fishing."

Today, five decades later, Chris owns the AZ Fly Shop in Phoenix, Arizona, and loves taking people of all ages and experiences on fishing expeditions all over the world.

What comes naturally to you? Perhaps there was a time you loved cooking, singing like a rock star in the shower, playing sports. Or maybe you're like my daughter (who is now an engineer) who built homes for her hamster out of cardboard boxes.

Start to speculate about what came naturally to you as a young child. Here are some examples:

- Making people laugh
- Seeing patterns in numbers and nature (e.g. the Fibonacci sequence)
- Being of service / doing things for others

Now, pick up a pen, and fill in the blanks.

What comes naturally to me is:

____

____

____

____

____

Feel free to come back to this exercise later if you think of more things that come naturally to you.

Encouragement (If You Need It)

I want you to know, as you begin to awaken to your purpose, you might find it daunting. Taking that first big step requires no small amount of courage. Don't be surprised if you notice some feelings that stop you from moving forward. For example, you might feel that you are too old. Or you might feel that you are too young. Maybe you've crossed paths with someone like Mrs. Turner, my secondary school English teacher, who told me, "You'll never make it."

We all have doubts or worries about our ability to succeed; we all have a fear that we "can't make it." Now is the time for you to pick up one foot and place it in front of the other, one step at a time.

This is not a race. Don't compare yourself with anyone else. This is about you and your purpose.

"If you're going through hell, keep going."
Winston Churchill

Remember: You don't need permission from me, Churchill, or anyone else, to be great!

"Enjoy the journey!"

Community

Chapter 2
The Second Foundational Framework

"Comparison is the thief of joy."
Theodore Roosevelt

Have you ever found yourself comparing yourself to others? Other people's bodies, cars, houses, education, relationships, happy family photographs, and their perfect selfies. In the world of comparison, you are living either a better-than life or a less-than life.

It's Friday evening. I'm slumped on the couch in front of a chick flick, thinking of absolutely nothing. I can hear my husband in the kitchen, muttering under his breath. His head is buried beneath the sink, as he works on fixing a blocked waste disposal. Now, here we have a married couple who have two completely different agendas; and neither is thinking of concluding the night with a romantic, candlelit waltz. Nothing about this scenario is noteworthy, brilliant, or shiny. Certainly not deserving of a selfie, a comment, or a thumbs up. Relax. I'll remind you again this is not a race. Who cares? Whether your life is under the sink or in your pajamas, you get to say what you want to create.

Transactions Exist in Community

In Chapter One, we introduced the subject of transactions. Let's now take a deeper dive into the world of transactions.

During the past several weeks, you have engaged in hundreds of transactions. For the most part, as you live your daily life, you don't give much thought to these transactions; they are automatic. In fact, unless you are doing something big (e.g. buying a car, moving to another city, getting married), you might not even notice the transactions. But life is made up of a long stream of tiny transactions. Try to recall some of them: signing up for a course, calling a contractor, paying a bill, scheduling an appointment, requesting a refund, navigating the security screening at the airport, and swiping your credit card.

Let's do an exercise. The intention of this exercise is to heighten your awareness of the transactions around you.

Look around the room you are in. For now, just pay attention to items that are smaller than a loaf of bread. (Ignore any items that are larger than a loaf of bread.) Pick one item that you love, an item that makes you happy when you look at it or pick it up.

Take a good look at this item that you love. Think about all the transactions that needed to happen before that item could end up in the room with you. Maybe you bought it yourself, or maybe it was a gift. Maybe it was made in a far-off factory, or maybe it was handcrafted by someone who loves you.

This item you love has a past!

It probably required dozens of transactions before the item finally arrived in the room with you. Some of those transactions directly involved you (i.e. you were a party to the transaction). On the other hand, some of the transactions happened without your involvement, possibly even without your knowledge.

Let's identify some of these transactions. First, look again at the item you love, and write at least three transactions that you were <u>directly involved in.</u>

1. _______________________________________

2. _______________________________________

3. _______________________________________

Now, write at least three transactions that happened without <u>your involvement.</u>

1. _______________________________________

2. _______________________________________

3. _______________________________________

This item you love, this item that makes you happy, did not come into your life in a vacuum. It came into your life via a series of transactions, all involving people. It was a community that brought this item to you.

The Transaction Trap

Are you starting to become more aware of transactions in your life?

There's something else to say about transactions: Some transactions turn out *good* (i.e. the way you want), and some transactions turn out *bad* (i.e. not the way you want). Let's explore the good and bad of transactions a bit.

When a transaction is completed, and it turns out good, it might give you a moment of satisfaction. And yet, in the next moment, you find yourself wanting more: more acknowledgment, more recognition, more approval. So here's the trap: Your successful transactions are short-lived satisfactions. The search for more approval, or more recognition, is not a true expression of who you are. It will not fulfill your purpose in life.

It's important to point out that the transaction, per se, is neither good nor bad. The trap comes when you are being driven by transactions. Are you noticing that you are unfulfilled, bored, tired, or even lonely? If so, consider that you are living a life that is driven by transactions.

Who Are You?

When I hear the question, "Who Are You?", there are certain answers that just pop up immediately. "I am Jeanne-Marie". "I am an artist". "I am English". And although these answers are correct, they are very limiting. These answers are very static, very much an end result. They reveal nothing about the process that brought me to where I am today.

As we examine the question, "Who Are You?", I will introduce you to an exercise that will give you a new way of looking at the question.

Fred McFeely Rogers, known professionally as Mister Rogers, was an American television host, author, producer, and Presbyterian minister. While delivering the 2002 Dartmouth College commencement address, he asked the graduating class to "think about those who have helped you become who you are today." Then he continued, "Let's just take a minute in honor of those who have cared about us all along the way."

What kind of people was Mister Rogers thinking of? It could be parents, a babysitter, a particular teacher, or possibly a favorite aunt. As you think about the people who have cared about you all along the way, try not to limit yourself. See if you can find someone outside of the usual groups.

Now it's time for you to do this exercise yourself. Open your notebook to a clean page and write the names that come to your mind. Use a timer to measure out 60 seconds, a full minute to honor those people.

Make sure you do this exercise before moving on. Some of us like to skip ahead. Do you notice certain times when you rush ahead before completing a prerequisite task?

What names did you write? Are you surprised by who showed up? Sometimes it was a person you were not so fond of, maybe a teacher from your very first school, or a person who served you coffee at your local café. And then there are names you did not write. It's all fine. The important part is to be present to those who have cared about you all along the way.

Shared Values

One of the rewarding benefits of a community is when you find yourself connected to that community's shared values. Sometimes, the shared value is an explicit part of the community. For example, many charitable organizations have a clearly stated vision or mission which reveals the values of the community. In such cases, possible shared values could be:

- Being of service
- Respect (or love) of animals
- Protection of the environment
- Providing educational scholarships

In other cases, the shared values of the community are not explicit. They might have developed informally over time. This is very common in a family setting. For instance, my mother was a very hard worker. After an eight-hour day working as a personal assistant, my mother returned home, prepared dinner for a family as a single parent, and then continued tirelessly sewing costumes for our dance competitions. I hardly ever saw my mother sleep. She liked to say, "You don't get nothing in life unless you work hard."

Nobody could match her work ethic. Today, my siblings still compete to see who works the hardest.

Although moving fast and busy about the house was applauded, reading was not. Did your family share the value of hard work? How about education? Maybe sports or physical activity? Were you encouraged to watch political debates? What about saving wounded animals or traveling? Notice some of these shared values are still with you today.

Embracing Community

Sometimes you need to proactively insert yourself into a community; or proactively draw the community toward you.

During a recent visit to Italy, it took a community to help me attend a soccer match. I had promised my friend Pasquale, who owns a café in Casale Monferrato, that I would watch him play an important match. The match was scheduled for the following Sunday, in the neighboring town of Trino. At first, it seemed like something I could do on my own. When I made the promise, I didn't think about how I would make the 10-mile trip to Trino, with no car. On the scheduled day, I confidently walked to the train station, only to find that trains and buses do not run in small towns in Italy on Sundays.

Now I had a choice to make. I could break my promise, or I could set aside my ego and ask for help.

I courageously reached out to Mikarla, a woman I had met just the day before. Mikarla speaks no English, but I managed to get my message across to her by text (with much assistance from Google Translate). Mikarla found a friend, Riccardo, who graciously agreed to drive me to the game. Riccardo showed up in his white Fiat 500 and off we drove! I got to keep my promise, thanks to the power of community.

In The Game

You might have suffered some childhood traumas: been bullied; been called fat; been shamed by friends who found out you wet your bed. Understandably, you lost trust in making good, solid friendships.

This is where you courageously pick up your baggage and boldly begin your mission of seeking great friendships in your community.

Try this on: Do you attend support groups for addictions or codependency? Yes? Then you have recovery as a shared value with that group. Perhaps you have found your place in spiritual, religious, meditation, or yoga groups. Perfect!

What about the gym, your local bank, neighborhood, café, or grocery store? These are all places where you can share your values with these communities.

We are in an exploration to find a place where you say you feel at home. For example, if you love animals and you own a dog, you might find a dog park in your neighborhood, or greet a dog owner while taking Fido for a walk. You'll probably learn all about Nova, Luna, and Siggy long before you find out about the doggy's owner's life. Regardless of what example you relate to, we are creating shared values in our own environment.

Who are the people in your life who are quite happy to support you being in the game? And, conversely, who are the ones who are not in the game, the ones who would rather you stay on the sidelines with them, so you can both complain about the game and avoid taking ownership of your life?

You want to start finding people in your community who are "in the game" with you.

Let's start first with a few examples to get you thinking about some people in various communities. Remember, these are examples, to get you thinking:

- Mini car owners wave to other Mini car owners, and find camaraderie at their community rallies.

- GoFundMe empowers communities to raise funds for a specific project or campaign.

- Parents whose kids play soccer bond on the sidelines and yell, "Gooooooal."

- Podcasters invite other podcasters to be guests on their show.

- Golf and Yoga are great ways to meet new people with similar interests.

- Motorcyclists can build long-lasting friendships on a Sunday cruise.

Regardless of where you were raised or your cultural background, now is the time for you to find your place in the world.

Distance Within a Community

Just as a community has the power to bring people together, we cannot escape the fact that communities also have the power to separate people. Have you noticed that some communities are more welcoming than others? Have you noticed that you don't feel "at home" in certain communities, even if those communities want to include you?

Like many children, I had trouble fitting into the community called "school".

I had long black hair with olive skin, in England during the 1970s, when immigration was on the rise, and racial prejudice was widespread. I was a Catholic in a Protestant country. I took weekly elocution lessons to minimize my lisp, repeatedly reciting "She sells seashells by the seashore" to my teacher, Mrs. Benfield.

I was different.

The other students called me "Blackie". My speech impediment was not a hit with the cool kids. Needless to say, I found out early how to keep my head down and pretend to "fit in", while feeling isolated. I stayed separate.

The question is: Where do you keep yourself separate or distant?

Finding Your Voice

A friend named Diane told me about attending her family reunion in Boston. Over those few days, she noticed that none of her family was recycling. She showed up as a committed environmentalist having recycled for years, and asked with an attitude, "Doesn't anyone recycle here?" Her uncle responded, "Nah, we don't bother with recycling." She had come to the reunion with a strong point of view. Of course, she believed recycling was the responsible thing to do. She felt disconnected from her family because they did not share the same values. Suddenly she had lost the purpose of being with her family. She was now in a transactional conversation about sustainability.

At that moment, Diane had a choice to create another context. She had an opportunity to create understanding, while still maintaining respect for others' points of view. What if Diane committed to being a source of information about recycling in her communities? Now there's a purpose bigger than her original reaction.

Instead of alienating the family (which you know is very possible), she begins to see a purpose greater than herself. She sees a possibility for action. She becomes the creator of a cleaner and healthier environment for future generations. *Now that's big!* And it can get even bigger. Imagine that she takes a stand as a steward of the planet. She joins a community that contributes to global efforts and addresses light pollution, climate change, and sustainable energy. And it all started with a conversation at a family gathering.

As we continue to work through the Second Foundational Framework, study the relationships you have with your community. Question who you naturally connect with and whether those people authentically bring you joy. Some of you have spent many years holding on to an identity that no longer fits you, only because of a commitment you once made. You are the only one who can give yourself permission to drop that cause and recommit to something that inspires you today. That could include friends, careers, and commitments that no longer serve you. Begin to honor your real self. Maybe that project or campaign no longer ignites you. Are you willing to let it go and give yourself permission to create a new purpose worthy of your life?

Now use your notebook and do some writing. List the people, projects, and commitments that no longer serve you.

____

____

____

____

____

Do not move on until you have completed the exercise above.

Now you have a choice to create what you really want. Find some people, find some friends, find a project that really ignites you.

Business of Real Estate

Chapter 3
The Third Foundational Framework

*"Out beyond ideas of wrongdoing, and rightdoing,
there is a field. I'll meet you there."*

Rumi

You could say that my fascination with real estate started at the age of ten. In the late 1970s, after my siblings left home, my mother became entrepreneurial, renting rooms to international students.

My weekly chores included providing clean utensils and supplies in the kitchen and bathroom. I often listened and watched as our lodgers performed prayers facing toward the Kaaba in Mecca. Some students who were living in our home gathered in the living room and talked about the civil unrest in a far-off land called Iran, sometimes called Persia.

Mohammed, Amir, Nazim, and others who were renting from my mother could not return to their homes in Iran for fear of being targeted and executed because of the demonstrations and protests against the Shah.

Who knew this was my introduction to the real estate industry, let alone the Middle East?

Elise

Decades later, when my husband and I met our real estate agent, Elise Kiely, there was something very special in her manner and interactions with our family. It was 2012, and we had many conversations about the kind of home we were looking for, and the kind of school that was important to our daughter, one of the remaining teenagers living at home.

If you are an agent, you might be thinking, of course, this is one of the integral methods of building a client relationship. However, how many clients really experience the agent fulfilling their needs ... beyond the transaction? Tim and I hemmed and hawed for three years before we found and settled into our new home in Maine in 2015. Elise remained patient, kind, and generous; she continued to do so years later, long after helping us sell that same home in Maine.

Elise had a vision, captured it, and has been running with her passion for over twenty years. In her own words, "In thinking about why I do what I do, I have come to appreciate being as actively engaged with my clients as I would with close friends and family. I make sure I provide more value than I could ever receive monetarily. I love to build relationships with individuals, couples, and families and be a large part of their new beginnings or the closing of a chapter in their lives. I believe agents are an integral and significant element of family life in America."

When people read what Elise has to say about her passion for real estate, many would say, "Of course", or "That's obvious". But is it obvious? Do most people engage in their careers with that kind of passion? When did we give up and become resigned to the belief that life is just about a transaction?

Many of us know people who are in the real estate industry: short-term rental owners; long-term rental owners; fix and flippers; real estate educators; agents. I have worked with many who genuinely care and who are truly committed and attentive beyond the transaction. But it's easy to fall into the trap of seeing the real estate industry as merely transactional, rather than as a vocation of self-expression. I would love more than anything to see you thrive and find your purpose; a purpose that inspires you to feeling fulfilled and being part of a legacy.

According to the National Association of Realtors (NAR), failure as a real estate agent is defined as acquiring a real estate license and then leaving the industry within five years. The NAR reports that 75% of real estate agents fail within the *first* year, and 87% fail within five years.

Many agents begin with hope, but they end their careers having never found a purpose beyond that first sale.

Inherited Beliefs

At Josh Linkner's company, ePrize, he often tells a fable, the "Meatloaf Story"[1].

---

1   The "Meatloaf Story" is reproduced here with the permission of the copyright owner, Josh Linkner.

A mother is making meatloaf with her teenage daughter; a ritual they've been doing together for years. As part of the tradition, the two chefs cut the ends of each side of the meatloaf before putting it in the oven. One day, the teen asks, "Mom, why do we cut the ends off the meatloaf before we put it in the oven?"

Taken by surprise, the mom began to think. She had no good reason, other than that's how her own mother did it and that was the way she learned. Together, the two called up grandma. "Grandma, why do we cut the ends off each side of the meatloaf before putting it in the oven?" After a brief laugh, the grandmother admitted that she didn't know the answer either. It was the way her own mother taught her. Tradition. It turns out her mother was living in a nearby nursing home, so they all went to visit.

Upon hearing the question, the 98-year-old great-grandmother roared with laughter. "I have no idea why you are cutting the ends off the meatloaf! I used to do it only because I didn't have a big enough pan!"

Understanding the evolution of one's beliefs is essential. Your beliefs are almost certainly influenced by your life experiences and the people around you. Nevertheless, it's important to discern between what genuinely originates from within you, and what is inherited from your parents and your parents' parents.

It's important to be aware of what is merely inherited, and then question if it truly aligns with your values. For example, your friend's fourteen-year-old daughter wishes to go on a vacation.

Your friend might believe that their teenager should pay for her own vacation. You, on the other hand, might have another opinion: Why burden the teenager with this monetary responsibility?

Many of our beliefs and opinions are inherited, i.e. handed down to us without question. The same can be said of your purpose. Ask yourself: Am I the creator of this purpose, or did it come from somebody else?

For several years, I drove to Boston from Maine to lead growth and development seminars. I drove three hours each way. On the way home, late at night, I invariably had to pull over and park at a 24-hour service station to take a thirty-minute cat nap. Even now, I have a stiff neck recalling those dark nights, resting my head against the driver's side window. One night, I had an epiphany. I realized that I was programmed to sleep in the car at a service station. I inherited my mother's belief against spending money to stay the night in a hotel. As a young child, I watched from the back seat as my mother pulled over to take naps at service stations while returning from camping trips. My mother would never pay to stay in a hotel in a million years. Without a second thought, I also would never pay to stay in a hotel. This was a default reaction. I was a product of inherited beliefs.

Now is your chance to write down some of your inherited beliefs. Although you may not have identified any of them yet, you still have them. To help you find them, you can try looking at places in your life where you want to fit in, such as at school, at work, or in social situations.

Below are some examples of inherited beliefs you may recognize.

- As a man, you are the sole breadwinner of the family.
- As a woman, your job is to take care of children and the home.
- In sports or business, if you don't win every time, you are a failure.
- Status symbols are important: a fancy car, a gold watch, a large house.
- We don't talk about our salary.

Now write some of your inherited beliefs. Are they from your parents, maybe an auntie, a teacher, your culture, a religion — even a book you read?

____

____

____

____

____

Intention Revisited

Waking up in the morning could be an invitation to pursue your purpose. However, often this is not our experience. I am reminding you once again to continue creating an intention. Some people wake up joyfully. Many others wake up berating themselves. You sent a bad email, you did not keep a promise, you should have more money in the bank, you should not have eaten that last chunk of cheese, and ugh that property should have sold last month. If you are not creating an intention, your mind wanders aimlessly, and has only one interest: keeping you safe and snuggled under your blanket to protect you from dinosaurs.

What is your intention, right now? Are you distracted? Did you start scrolling for approval on your cell phone? Even if you have not discovered your purpose, you can create an intention right now. I'll ask again what is your intention right now — *at this moment?* I'm not talking about a list of things to do; I'm talking about a creative intention.

My husband and I once owned a small house in Pennsylvania, which we rented to a wonderful family of four. After a couple of years, they expressed interest in purchasing the house, but were hesitant about the sale price. The potential buyers asked us if we would lower the purchase price, to which we responded that we were not willing to go below the market value. I could hear them clearly getting annoyed. I also started getting irritated by the negotiation process. It took everything for me to stay in the conversation. Then suddenly I realized I had no intention other than to react to the request of lowering the price. As soon as I asked myself, "What is my intention?", it became simple. I created the intention that the buyers have a great experience.

I realized that their concerns were not solely about money, but were rooted in the fear of taking on a big commitment and owning their first home. Instead of focusing on the transactional aspect, we could now acknowledge that this was a big adventure. "I totally understand where you're coming from; of course you should be freaking out!" The moment I said that, there was a pause, and the tension started to melt away.

By acknowledging their underlying emotions, I could address their actual concerns. The transactional relationship became intentional, with a bigger purpose. Notice though, I had to pause and reflect not just on the words she was saying, but what she was not saying: "I'm scared of making a mistake."

Take the time to look beyond your surface-level conversation and really listen to what people are not saying, and yet are expressing. This can help you gain a better understanding of your own obstacles.

The key was to be present in the moment, be in the now, and approach each interaction as a unique opportunity for both parties.

Overview of Infrastructure

Simply said, you are not alone. You may feel like you are working on your own; but consider that you are navigating along your life's journey within a vast existing infrastructure. When you hear this word, you might immediately think of roads, bridges, rails, or waterways, all designed to transport raw material, finished goods, and people. However, there's much more to explore here. The purpose here is to reveal the interdependence we have with various infrastructures that support our mission and our purpose.

The most common infrastructure groups you may recognize:
- Transportation
- Personal and Business
- Environmental
- Economic

Transportation Infrastructure

In 2021, worldwide e-commerce sales totaled about $5 trillion. This would not be possible without the complex interconnected infrastructure of roads, bridges, railways, and navigable waterways. On top of that, all these transportation routes would be useless without delivery drivers, railroad operators, pilots, and sea captains.

As you continue to read, reflect on where in your life these infrastructures play a role, either in your business or in your personal life. Notice the pervasiveness of infrastructure. Appreciate how that infrastructure supports your mission.

It's easy to think, "I did this all on my own!" However, you cannot operate a business without infrastructure. The same is true in your personal life; you haven't journeyed alone. This conversation is way bigger than you or me. Isn't it uplifting to know that you are not alone?

Whether you are aware of it or not, you are part of a larger collective system. You exist in a community, a neighborhood, a municipality, a country, and so on

Personal and Business Infrastructure

What happens when something goes awry in your life? What infrastructure supports you? Perhaps you need the infrastructure of the police, or the courts. These provide support in times of crisis, or when there is a disagreement.

As we move through the 21st century, we are dramatically expanding our use of telephone networks and the Internet. We use these elements of infrastructure to expand productivity in our businesses. For example, many workers use video conferencing to meet with colleagues or clients across the globe.

If you focus solely on the video conferencing infrastructure, you'll see that it consists primarily of cameras, customized software, plus remote computer servers. But those elements depend on other layers of infrastructure that already exist, most notably the Internet. And then, looking at the next layer, you'll see that the Internet itself depends on (among other things) a vast reliable electricity grid. And even the grid depends on further layers of infrastructure. It's infrastructure all the way down!

The importance of infrastructure becomes apparent when it breaks or is absent. It's easy to overlook the existence and significance of infrastructure until we encounter disruptions or limitations in its functioning.

Environmental Infrastructure

This one may not be on your mind every day. However, there are many organizations and people that are integral to our health and well-being.

Consider the Environmental Protection Agency (EPA), a part of the US federal government. The EPA is a part of the infrastructure that works to ensure, among other things, that Americans have clean air, land, and water.

Have you heard of the National Fire Protection Association (NFPA)? Although the name might suggest that it's a government organization, it is not. The NFPA is an international nonprofit organization, based in the US, devoted to eliminating death, injury, and property loss due to fire, electrical, and related hazards. Throughout the world, 10,000 volunteers study these hazards, and they work to publish safety codes and best practices documents. While the NFPA itself doesn't have any regulatory authority, their standards have been adopted by many government agencies.

In England, the National Health Service is part of the government-funded healthcare infrastructure. The founding principles were that health services should be comprehensive, universal, and free at the point of delivery — a health service based on clinical need, not ability to pay. This is an example of an infrastructure that the people in England are well aware of, interacting with it regularly.

In the US, the Centers for Disease Control and Prevention (CDC) has the aim of protecting America from health, safety, and security threats. Although most Americans will never interact directly with the CDC, the activities of the CDC are a key part of the US public health infrastructure.

Economic Infrastructure

Have you ever thought about the mortgage market as an infrastructure? Many of us reading this will remember The Great Recession, due to mortgage delinquencies, foreclosures, and devaluation of housing-related securities. This reduced household spending and business investment, causing an economic downturn and a global financial crisis.

Economic infrastructure refers to the systems and mechanisms that support the economy. Examples of this are the banks of a country. In the US, the banking system infrastructure also includes the Federal Reserve System, and the Federal Deposit Insurance Corporation (FDIC). These government organizations have multiple responsibilities, but a primary focus is establishing policies that maintain confidence in the banking system as a whole.

Infrastructure in a business setting extends beyond individual efforts, involving the contributions of neighbors, transportation, and various support networks. An example of an economic infrastructure that contributed to the community is Andrew Carnegie's library. He donated $300,000 to build The Washington Public Library, in Washington, DC, back in 1903.

Summary

You are not walking around on this planet on your own. You did not create this business or this life on your own. Your parents brought you here. The infrastructure of transportation got you here.

Your community infrastructure created involvement, passion, and diversity. The environmental and economic infrastructures help keep you safe and healthy while you navigate your personal and professional life.

Do you still believe you are on your own?

What are the infrastructures in your personal life?

____

____

____

____

____

What are the infrastructures in your business life?

____

____

____

____

If you want to go into more detail, I recommend reading *How Infrastructure Works*, by Deb Chachra, PhD, Professor of Engineering, Olin College of Engineering.

Money

Chapter 4
The Fourth Foundational Framework

"What we really want to do is what we are really meant to do. When we do what we are meant to do, money comes to us, doors open for us, we feel useful, and the work we do feels like play to us."

Julia Cameron

A month before my mother died, I flew to Ballarat, an old gold rush town outside of Melbourne, Australia, to sort through her belongings. She had several large cardboard boxes of stuff that she had collected for over fifty years. There were letters from her parents and friends, airmail from her sisters, plus other assorted souvenirs from my siblings and me, accumulated over the years. I saw an overwhelming number of old black and white photographs, stained from life, strapped in albums. Hundreds of lost bits, kept here in the hope of one day finding the other bits; broken ornaments, a jumble of woven and knitted fabrics that were once vibrant but now due for a power wash; bags of black Super 8 film reels of our music and dance competitions.

I spent several tedious, painful days going through boxes with my mother, who now was struggling with dementia. She stared at each item with a certain hollow gaze. Just like the gaze I have when attempting to make sense of a car owner's manual after the "check engine" light appears. Hours went by, going through the motions of piecing together a life that once was. Occasionally I would get up and let out a weep of despair in the rest home's public bathroom.

We mistakenly think that life is about more "moolah". But that thought undermines the value of your life. When you lose a loved one, in those moments of grief, your thoughts do not turn to Benjamin Franklin or George Washington. There's a significant risk that comes with believing that accumulating wealth is our life's ultimate purpose. While money is important for transactions and obligations, it shouldn't equate to life's purpose, nor be seen as something we inherently need.

Legal Tender

When my husband and I were touring parts of Colombia, we were frequently approached by young children asking for money. Some people would say they were begging for money. However, they were neither begging nor demanding. They simply had their hands outstretched, with an absent look in their eyes. It's as if they knew that it was important to get money from the tourists. So that's what they did.

At one point we ran out of pesos. We could only give them American dollar bills. Children suddenly appeared from everywhere and were so thrilled to receive money. However, for these children, receiving American currency was useless. The pieces of paper looked pretty in their hands, but there was no place to spend it.

Monopoly

What is your first memory of money? Did your parents give you a weekly allowance? How was money talked about in your formative years? Personally, when I was a kid, I thought everything was free. After all, I wasn't paying. The adults around me used to say, "Money doesn't grow on trees." I never once looked outside our kitchen window to confirm such an absurd remark.

At a certain age, I started receiving money in envelopes, and inside birthday cards. It was clear, from my siblings' reactions, that money was way more important than the kind words printed on the card. We touched on this earlier, in Chapter Three … the beginning of an inherited belief.

When I was six years old, my brothers and sisters taught me to play the British version of Monopoly. Most of you know the object of any game is to win! In Monopoly, the strategies for winning look like this: You have to spend money quickly, earn money by renting out your plastic houses, plan for the unexpected, start saving early, stay out of jail, and negotiate. I have a memory of being good at most aspects of the game, except one: negotiating.

During one of our Monopoly sessions, my game token landed on Liverpool Street. Before I knew what was happening, the property went to auction, because anything can happen when you're six years old! My siblings kept bidding up the price, and

I ended up purchasing the property at a much higher cost. My first memory of money was being ripped off. I was conned. I was taken advantage of. Although it was only a game, it permanently left an impression.

Now it's your turn. Open to a new page in your notebook. Take some time to write your first recollections of money.

____

____

____

____

____

Are you experiencing some emotions? Maybe you saw a flickering moment, or maybe you saw an entire series of events.

How was money discussed in your family? Maybe you had to save for what you wanted. Or maybe money was plentiful, and you could have anything you asked for. Were there rules (maybe a silent agreement) about how you should behave when you received money?

Can you see that money serves as a measure and an evaluation? In our world, our net worth is often confused with our self-worth. What can we do to free ourselves from this obsessive idea?

The Value of Money

Money, while basically transactional, can lead to opportunities.

At a local swim meet, a father was waiting impatiently in line to watch his daughter swim the 50M butterfly heat. He was causing a bit of a stir with the other parents. He was rude and loud; a perfect demonstration of how we tell our kids not to behave in line. The line was moving at a snail's pace. Over the intercom, he heard his daughter's race being announced. He ran up to the front, demanding to be let in first. To everyone's annoyance, they let him in. The father was asked for the eight dollar admission fee, in cash, to which he replied that he only had a credit card. Imagine the tension.

Then, at the back of the line, a mother appeared and said, "Don't worry, go see your daughter swim. I've got this." The impatient man's demeanor softened as he accepted the cash and promised to pay her back. He was surprised that another parent could be so understanding and generous. Was this brief exchange about money or generosity?

Money, in and of itself, is useless on its own; but it becomes meaningful the moment it facilitates a connection with another. The father did not need the money; but he certainly needed someone else's understanding. The eight dollars was an opportunity to be generous. It went "beyond the transaction"; it transformed the experience.

However, sometimes we can fall into the money trap. What starts as an act of generosity may result in expectations and resentments. The so-called generous mother spent months waiting for the return of her eight dollars. It was not about the cash, but about her belief that she could not trust anyone; she had lost faith in people to keep their promises. Her loss of faith was more damaging than if she had given the father fifty thousand dollars.

Sometimes in life, things happen that drive up bad feelings about money. You might feel *regret* over a purchase that you didn't think through fully. You might feel *anger* after paying for poor service or shoddy workmanship. You might feel *resentment* if you lend someone money, and they never pay you back.

Take some time to write about some financial situations that have you feeling regret, anger, or resentment.

____

____

____

____

____

Now, let's start to turn this around. You don't have to be stuck with those negative feelings! You can take action to reach a resolution.

If you lent someone money, and they never talked about paying it back, you could ask them about it. "Are you going to pay me back?" It would be great if they said yes. But if they say no, you don't have to keep guessing. You could even decide to call it a "gift".

If you bought something that you now regret, perhaps you could sell it. Even if you take a loss, just having that thing out of your life might give you some peace.

Here's a chance for you to be creative. Take another look at the financial situations you just wrote about. What actions could you take that would have you start to feel resolved in your life?

____

____

____

____

____

Legacy

Chapter 5
The Fifth Foundational Framework

"The best way to predict your future is to create it."
Abraham Lincoln

This conversation intends to start the work of building a legacy that inspires you. With the rare exception, most people are not born with a preexisting legacy, such as the Rockefellers, Kennedys, Vanderbilts, and the British royal family. Most of us mere mortals are concerned with our essential needs. Thinking beyond those basic needs, and striving for a legacy, requires attention and intention.

Variety Is the Spice

Your legacy can take many forms. It could be large, or small. It could be well-known, or low-profile. It could impact a large group of people, or a small, focused group. There is no wrong kind of legacy, as long as it inspires you.

The first thing we will do is discuss a sampling of different legacies. This is not meant to box you in, but rather is intended to spark your creative ideas.

We'll start with some legacies that have been around for a while and are generally well-known.

- **<u>Nobel Foundation:</u>** This is a private institution that administers the various Nobel Prizes (e.g. the Nobel Peace Prize). This foundation was established by Alfred Nobel, the inventor of dynamite. The conventional understanding is that Nobel was concerned about how he would be remembered (as someone who profited from the munitions industry), and he therefore established an organization to honor those who work for peace.

- **<u>St. Jude Children's Research Hospital:</u>** This is a non-profit medical facility, founded in 1962 by entertainer Danny Thomas. This institution provides free treatment to children who have catastrophic diseases such as cancer. Thomas decided to start this hospital to honor the New Testament Apostle Saint Jude Thaddeus. Thomas credited Saint Jude with answering his prayers at a time when Thomas was unable to financially provide for his family.

There are some legacies that are not an organization or a physical structure. Instead, they are a memory of someone's heroic or groundbreaking actions.

- **<u>Sir Nicholas Winton:</u>** A British stockbroker who helped rescue Jewish children from Czechoslovakia in the months leading up to World War II. Most of these children were refugees from Nazi Germany and were in danger of being sent to concentration camps. Thanks to Winton's efforts, 669 of these children were relocated to homes in Britain.

- **<u>Rachel Carson:</u>** A marine biologist and environmental activist. Her 1962 book, Silent Spring, addressed the dangers of indiscriminate pesticide use. Her work is often credited with sparking the modern environmental movement.

Many of the legacies listed in this chapter have been around for a long time, and their founders have died. In contrast, here are some legacies that are more recent, and their founders are still alive.

- **<u>Women Business Founders' Endowed Scholarship Fund:</u>** This scholarship supports University of Washington (UW) undergraduate students (in the Civil & Environmental Engineering Department) who are passionate about advancing the interests of women in the engineering field, especially the business side of engineering. This scholarship was established by three UW Engineering graduates, Amy Haugerud, Anne Symonds, and Kristen Betty.

- **<u>Infant Club Foot Appeal (ICA):</u>** This is a medical charity that provides facilities and treatment for children with the birth defect known as Club Foot. ICA was founded in 2010 by Dr. Charlotte Hawkins, and operates primarily on the African island of Zanzibar. Dr Hawkins, a specialist in lower limb pediatrics in London, was inspired to set up ICA after witnessing the scale of the problem in Zanzibar.

Here are a few other legacies that don't fit into any specific category.

- **<u>Oprah Winfrey Leadership Academy for Girls:</u>** This is an all-girls boarding school (grades 8 through 12) in South Africa. The mission of the school is to provide a nurturing educational environment for academically gifted girls who come from disadvantaged backgrounds. The students are prepared for leadership positions in South Africa or abroad. This school was founded by media personality Oprah Winfrey in 2007.

- **<u>Rotary International:</u>** This is one of the world's largest service organizations. It was founded in 1905 by Paul Harris. Rotary International members participate in a wide range of charitable and humanitarian activities. Rotary is dedicated to causes that build international relationships, improve lives, and create a better world, all in support of their efforts toward peace and the eradication of polio.

- **<u>Al-Anon:</u>** This is an international organization that offers a program of recovery for the families and friends of alcoholics. It was founded in 1951 by Anne B and Lois W (the wife of the founder of Alcoholics Anonymous, Bill W).

Take Your Own Road

How can you reignite your purpose and align it with your desire to leave a lasting legacy? There are limitless opportunities. Maybe you want to leave a legacy to save animals from being euthanized. Or maybe the most important thing for you is to create a legacy for your family. When we're speculating about a legacy, we tend to get caught up in thoughts like, I need millions of dollars, or I don't have the time to start. But remember: People in your community are your biggest resources. Let your purpose unfold. When seeking a purpose, go beyond the transactions and explore what brings you joy.

Take your pen and notebook and speculate on how you would like to be known and what you would like to create today?

What do you need? This list might seem endless. Just start by writing three needs.

For example:
- I need to set up a meeting with some friends to talk about my idea.
- I need to research grants in my town or state.
- I need to listen to a podcast about my subject of interest.

In my early career, I painted large murals and created mosaics. My business partner, Susan Beresford, and I worked tirelessly with communities, schools, and cities. We initiated 120 projects over 20 years. We believed our art would remain on those walls for a lifetime, with people admiring the splashes of color and the clever designs. Families would cherish the lasting memories created during their involvement, fondly reminiscing about their artistic accomplishments for years to come.

Yet, as I revisit those familiar locations and stroll through subways or wander the streets where countless hours were spent priming, designing, and executing those projects, I'm disheartened to find walls defaced with graffiti or once beautiful mosaics destroyed. Despite the challenges, there are still a few murals that stand the test of time, resilient even after two decades, though they require ongoing maintenance to preserve their beauty.

But all said and done, it was always the people who really mattered. Gary, an enthusiastic volunteer on one of our London subway mural projects, was illiterate. At the age of forty-one, he went back to school to learn how to read and write. He was inspired after carefully painting letters on one of the mural projects. Gary no longer lives in a parking lot near East Croydon station; he now has a place he calls home. Then there was Paula, who had been depressed for years, working as a receptionist. While helping create the marketing for a project launch, she discovered she was a writer. She now publishes her articles in her local community newsletter.

Your connections between you and your communities, your families, and the people in your neighborhood are more than transactions. Consider your life a work of art, with intricate designs, and a splash of color.

Think of life as a dinner party. Often, we are compelled to know every detail of how it will turn out. We think we need to be in control of every detail of the menu. We want to know that the guests will behave in a particular way. We even expect the weather to be perfect. Have faith: Even though we cannot know these things, it will all turn out.

We have come to the end of this road together. Participating in the exercises has allowed us to share our stories. As we looked back at our lives, we found moments that provided us joy. Here are some joyful moments for me: the time my husband cried when his team won the Champions League; when my daughter was accepted into the college of her choice; my sister's first piano recital at the age of 60; the time I bathed a fifty-year-old rescued elephant in Sri Lanka. We can create purpose, moment by moment, and at any time.

You've come this far, and it's time to live the way you were meant to. It does not matter what you do, only that you are creating moment by moment. You are in the driver's seat.

Final Thoughts

*"There's only one person in the whole world
that's like you, and that's you. And people can
like you just exactly the way you are."*
Fred McFeely Rogers (Mister Rogers)

You now have *The Five Foundational Frameworks*. You have started your walk home.

Epilogue

I wholeheartedly thank you for investing in yourself. It has been an honor to walk you home. I look forward to hearing how you are transforming your life and leaving a legacy.

Jeanne-Marie Eayrs offers these programs and resources designed to elevate your performance:

- *The Ten Conversations™*: A modern transformational coaching model, delivered via video conference

- Speaking Engagements: Interactive and thought-provoking; designed to get your group to take action and cause results

- High-Performance Coaching: Customized training, designed to release your group's unlimited potential

For more information, visit: www.JeanneMarieEayrs.com

LinkedIn: www.linkedin.com/in/jeanne-marie-eayrs

Namaste

About the Author

Jeanne-Marie Eayrs was born in Kent, England, and emigrated to Australia as a teenager. In her early twenties, she moved to New York to study theater. She worked as a public artist for two decades. She loves real estate and is a real estate investor. Nearly twenty years ago, Jeanne-Marie discovered her passion for coaching. She has impacted thousands of people through conferences, live seminars, and online events.

Her adult children live in the United States. Jeanne-Marie lives with her husband, Tim, and a Rhodesian Ridgeback named Blue. They divide their time between their homes in Casale Monferrato, Italy, and Scottsdale, Arizona.

www.ingramcontent.com/pod-product-compliance
Lightning Source LLC
Chambersburg PA
CBHW061431050726
47593CB00006B/2314